Bridges

By Nick Rebman

SPARKS

Picture Glossary

bridges 4

cover 12

river 10

trains 6

Bridges help people.

People can go over things.

bridge

This bridge is for trains.

The bridge goes over the trees.

train

This bridge is for cars.

The bridge goes over a road.

car

This bridge is for bikes.

The bridge goes over a river.

river

This bridge has a cover.

The cover goes over the bridge.

cover

Bridges help people.

Cars and trucks go on this bridge.

busy

Do You Know?

This bridge is for ______.

people

cars

trains

bikes